Garden Walks:
Hand In Hand

Poems to Relax By

Gary W. Burns

Turning Corner Books ™

WWW.TURNINGCORNERBOOKS.COM

Copyright © 2010 by Vista View Publishing
P.O. Box 121, Haymarket, VA 20168

Library of Congress Catalog Card Number: 2010927197
ISBN: 978-0-9845342-3-4

Sixth Printing, May 2018

Manufactured in the United States
Designed by the author; artwork by the author.

Photos -
Jacket:
Front: Japanese Foot Bridge, Golden Gate Park, San Francisco,
California by the Author
Back: Lotus Flower Kenilworth Aquatic Gardens,
Washington DC by the Author

Page 62: Autumn Walk, by James W. Godwin

Other Books of Poetry
by Gary W. Burns

Bridges: To There (Poems for the Mind, Body & Spirit)

Clouds: On the Wind (Poems for the Soul – A Meditation)

Earth Tones: A Journey (Poetry for the Journey)

Moments: This to the Next (Poetry - Now and Eternity)

Poems of Love: A Selection

Rainy Day: Wondering (Poems for a Rainy Day)

To You With Love: Selected Poems

Twilight: Awaking the Stars (Poems of the Night's Light)

To Linda Marie

for her care
of all things

ೞ ━━━━━━━━━━ ೬

CONTENTS

❖ **Colorful Blooms**

i

❖ This Backyard Garden

❖ Garden Paths

❖ Seasons Cascading

❖ Perennial Days

Colorful Blooms

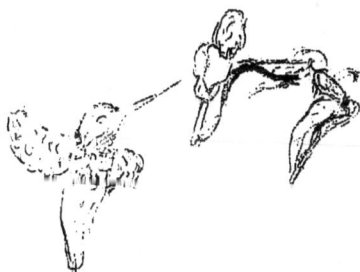

I'm fighting off
Winters' ward:
Its frosty scene,
And its
Hoary horde.

"Spring"

Spring's Bouquet

Yellow sun,
Golden rays
Streaming,
Billowing clouds
Lit bright
By morning;

Dawn
Calm
And colorful;

Snow
Melting away;

The day

Beginning:

Beautiful.

Wild Flowers

When I look without
And all is free,

When I look within
And all is simplicity,

Surely heaven
It will be.

We are all
Wild flowers

Growing
In the field
Of eternity.

Come In

1

At the open gate
Marigolds
All dressed up
In school-bus yellow
Say hello.

2

Along the stone walk
Nasturtiums
In a whirlwind romance
Dance;
Turning
With the wind and sun
Till the music's done.

3

All sunny day long
The hurrying bees
Rush
To the many-colored
Zinnias
Plush.

4

Just over there
A star
Of rich-rose
Rosie O'day
Novas between
Dragons of snapping
And roses of love.

5

Along the wall
In red-ablaze
Asters
Bask
All day
In weather
What may.

6

Welcome,
To my garden.

Today in the Rain

As we walked
Through the rain

You
Turned raindrops
In to love;

Me
I fell deeply.

Window

Through
     the window
Of
    my eye
The
    yellow rose
I
     do spy.
From
    the knowing
Of
    my why
I
    see through
This
    Loving I.

In Bloom

Mid-June:
I watch the marigolds,
   while the wait,
Late
     was I
     to plant them.

Mid-August:
With the backyard
In a wealth of bloom

Who would ever
     want to leave
The contentment
    of this
      flower-rich
        garden.

O So Fair

The butterfly
Winging
Against the sky
Is this worlds
Softest
Lullaby.

The First Marigold

I've picked
      the first marigold
            today.
Its solitary figure
      fills a small
            white vase.
Outside in the sunshine
      on its mother
      grows another
      and another
To take its place.

While here in the corner
      it shows
      the peacefulness
            of Grace.

The Songsmith

When I was twenty-two
                    tulips grew
Where dragons
                    now grow.
The tulips grew
                    five to a cluster
Where the snappers
                    now grow in a row.

Over
            at the gardens edge
One gladiatorial
                    gladiolus
                    does still remain
A companion
            of my twenty-second
                                year
It blooms once again
                as life's
                        poetic refrain.

Lilacs
And Memories

Memories of when
I was nine or ten:

Then it was
That the lilacs'
Purple bloom
Draped
The open side
Of the old
Half covered well.

And there it was,
When trouble came,
The farm ducks
Would run to hide.

When troubles come,
I recall memories
Of then

And
The care-free-ness
Of nine or ten.

The Living Room

In the living room
This afternoon;

Purple violets,
   serene-in-silence,
    enjoy the moment.
As the music
           of the day
Plays.

Still,
Cactus,
 in an ever repose,
   make not a move.

While all the while

Ivy

       in green hunger
                snaps
At the empty spaces
        it quickly
              engulfs.

This Backyard Garden

Flowers Everywhere

The asters,
Red capped
And green caped,
Stand vigilant.
Ready
To ladder over
The garden wall,
Should they get
The urgent call.

Me,
I lie
Not stand,
I'm neither capped
Nor caped
Nor shirted or with shoes:
I believe my cat sleeps
More than I do.
The neighbor's pups
Roust about.

With flowers everywhere,
How wonderful
This backyard garden.

Live

The heads keep falling off
The snapdragons

And graciously,

The end table
Keeps catching them.

The children are playing
In the rain,

I believe I'll go out
And do the same.

Full orchestra, first 3 stanzas
Strings plucked and flute last 2 stanzas

You
Holding Me

Know
That
As you
Hold me
I Love You

Know
That
As you
Lay me down
I Love You

Know
That
As you
Walk away
I Love You

Forever and a day
I Love You

Your Birthday

The carnations
    didn't come
    from my green thumb.
They were store bought
    and there brought
    to be pink, red, and white.

Happy Birthday
    from a dozen
    fern laced carnations
And me.

The Vase of Zinnias

The zinnias spread
Through the shades of red

There's one
So rich in red
You'd think it gold

And three
Pinkly-bold

Some
Are shades-of-red-off
Some
Are shades-of-red-on

Of all of them
I'm

So very fond

If I Were

1

If I were the morning
What would I do . . .

For you

I'd lift the veil of drowsy sleep
That keeps
You away from me,
Clear away dreams
That stayed too long,
And hold you softly
As the birds
Sing their morning song.

If I were the morning,
I'd give away my day
To you, wishing
You'd want me more
And adore
My garb of silver-blue.

For sure
I'd give the night its due
But always hoping, again
I'd see you.

2

If I were the night
What would I do . . .

For you

As the ocean of the universe
Ebbed and flowed
In celestial sway

I'd hold you tenderly
Till light came to day.

And I'd dream with you,
Knowing
Dreams come true.

3

Of course,
I'm not the morning
Nor the night
But I love you
As dearly as
Morning loves light
And stars
Love night.

Forget-Me-Not

Don't let words
Be hidden behind

Allow
No mask

Be

Love

All Day Long

On the plush end
Of a three foot stem

All day long
The honey bees
Push and pull
In and out

Gathering
Yellow

From the many fold
Petals
Of the marigold

On Your Way

Touch
Softly

Hold
Gently

Care
Warmly

Give
Easily

Love

Along With You

I'm
      not sure
Where I'm going
        but,
        I'm sure
I'm going
      Along With You.

Wind Dance

Standing tall
Alongside
The garden wall

The eager
        snapdragons,

All dressed
In graceful elegance,

Await
The whirling wind
To pay a call
And begin
The Wind Dance Ball.

Amid
Changing Hues

Greeting
The ever elegant
                    morning
The sun
All glorious and gold
     stretches wide
Across
The late autumn horizon.

As amid
     changing hues
Sunrays
         set aglow
The gossamer frost
   that runs
       the fence row.

Dear Love

You
The quiet one
There

Come
    to here,
        please.

Here
    to love
            dear.

Come near,
Make
    my heart
        complete.

Masterwork

Windows
Are living canvases

So what about
   the windows
        of your eyes

While
In Your Arms

Drown me
In Love,
And if you do
Hear a cry
You hear the joy
I sigh.

Lovingly

We can feel Love
But
We can't touch it;

Love touches us.

You
Touching me
Lovingly,
Me
Touching you
Lovingly too.

With You Now

When I was young
Lying by the stream
Looking up at the clouds

I was everywhere
And nowhere
In particular.

But even then
I knew
I was with you.

And Always

Let's lie down
In some field
Green.

Let's walk along some hillside
Then on
Through a flowered meadow.

Let's go up,
Up a flight of stairs,
Or two,
To somewhere high
Above the noisy city
Away from nameless crowds.

Let's stroll along
Some windswept shore.

Let's be together
Always.

Garden Paths

Healdsburg, CA

I'll Be Here

Look me over,

Hold me

When you've enough
Let me go - walk away.

I've only these words
To hold you:

If on those days
When gentleness sways
By chance you choose
To come to me again,
I'll be here.

Our Cares

Before we know it
Cold
Will make its way
Through summers house
And in its wake
Quickly close
The warm weather
Windows.

When that time is here
You'll say, 'Dear,
Light a fire'.

And as the flickering
Of the fire light
Casts dancing shadows
I'll pour wine,
We'll talk,
And share our cares.

O Gusty Wind

The day was not long
   in its passing
And though near death
   they were
The nasturtiums wished
   still to stand.

"Gust!" said the foe
  "away you go."

Let me be,
Let me be.

No matter the plea,
Strong was the foe,
  "Gust, blow!"

Away they go
    O . . .

The Crossing

As a child
I'd walk through the woods
And over the fields.

At times,
There'd be rivers
And streams to cross.

As a man
I've walked through dark,
Dark woods
And over wide, wide fields,
And oh
While going along
Life's highways
And byways
The rivers and streams
I've crossed.

All of us, always
Going along;
And oh
The rivers,
And field,
And streams
We cross.

Deep In Autumn

Summers'
　　　green noon
　　　　is long past
　　　and soon
　　　　　the last
Of the colorful
　　flowers
Will go
　to a secret place
　　to hide
　　from winters
　　mournful winds.

And there
　　　　await
Spring to open
Blossoms' Gate.

Love's Haven

While being tossed
        here and there
The petals of the pink rose
        paddle their way
        through the unseen air.
Up, down, then around
        they make their way
        to the wistful ground
As the sea they're in
                is stirred
        by the sightless wind.
Settled,
The pink ships
        harbor
        in the tall green grass;
Haven.

Ever so
        we are tossed
        and turned
In the sea
        of life
And through Love
Know of the tall green grass;

Haven.

Me
And You

Some say

Walking away
I say

Walking to

There goes
       me
And there goes
       You . . .

My Flower

No, there's never enough
                    time
To do all of the things
                    you want
I'd like to sit
            and watch
The rose
    come to curious bloom
But that would take
                all day
And I have to make Love
            to you by noon
                My Flower

Now:
Love

Heart to heart
And hand
In hand

Together
Let's walk

We can talk

Some-other-time

Love's Everywhere

Love is the warmth

In the glimmer
Of an eye

Love's everywhere

Enjoy

Sparrow & Rose

At sunset
A sparrow rest
Upon the stem
Of a summer rose.

Both light
In shade and color
Their easiness flows
From the gray
Of the garden wall.

In my imperfection
I detect no flaw.

The sparrow wings
The branch swings
To then fro,
To then fro.

And
Even though
They will never know,

Wherever they may go

Forever
Once
They were one

The sparrow
And the rose.

The Garden Nova

Colored with the bright
The earth holds tight
From spring till fall
The garden nova
Lit all.

What a time we had
The colors and me
As the sun
Steadily
Coaxed splendor
To the scenery.

Now,
Snowflakes
Have fallen enough
To hide
The green of the grass
Leaving winding curves
For the wandering eye.

Standing Silhouette

Standing silhouette
Against
The dusk of dawn
Naked limbed trees
Covered by ice
Surrounded
By snow
Mark the day.

No flower
Weathers this weather
As well
As the flower Love.

I Love You.

Oak Tree
Georgia
Jan, 1993

Seasons Cascading

Our Garden

I live in a garden

A garden
Of seasons

That bloom, and bloom
And bloom

Outside my window
Or in my room

April, May, June

Mid-October

And in December too

Warm, hot
Cool, cold

Outside my window
Or in my room

I live in a garden
Bloom after bloom

Another Year Gone

The year
Has come and gone

I can't say any of the seasons
Took me by surprise

But they took me
And you too

A bit further down the road
As seasons always do

Live

Profoundly
Simple

Harmony

Watching Leaves

1

I am still
Watching
Falling leaves
And August trees,
Thinking of you.

It's late August.

2

I notice the poplar trees
Lose their leaves early.

Apparently,
The departing leaves
No longer want
Nor need
To hold on.

3

Some trees
Keep their leaves
Long into winter
And some
Keep them
All winter long.

But,
I won't say,
Necessarily,
Those leaves are stronger
Than those
Of the poplar tree.

Perhaps,
They're simply
More willing to stay
Awhile longer.

4

Stay
Awhile longer,
Please.

Let's watch
The falling leaves.

Sometimes
Sorrows

1

Where is the rain
Now that I need it
To drown these sorrows?

I guess,
Out happy somewhere
Watering flowers
Or perhaps

Giving the sea blue
Its due.

2

Sometimes
Sorrows
Like the rains
Just keep falling.

Maybe
Like the rain on the flowers
We grow from our sorrows.

Surely,
We grow older by them.

3

Where's the rain

Now
That I need it . . .

So All Things

As winter
Drifts to their side
The frost flowers
Red, in their nakedness
Have no place to hide.

Discovery

A fresh day
Moving
Out of a stale night

Now
With clouds billowing
Where once
There was dark

The searching
Is done

In me
I discovered
You

And I've come
To understand
That by you
I know me
Deeply

Perennial Days

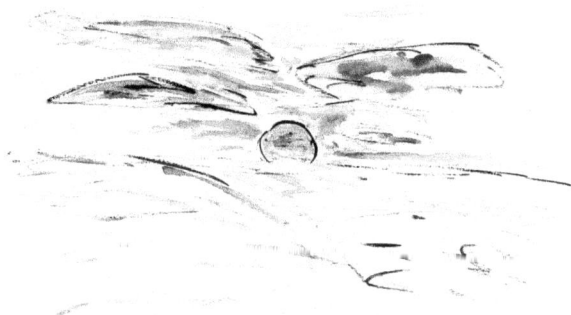

In the Air

I know
There's music in the air –
I've seen the sun
        tap dancing
            atop the sea,
The wind
            whirl in a waltz
        with the desert sand,
And autumn's golden wheat
                gently sway
                with the breeze
On an autumn day.

Everywhere,

There's music
In the air.

The Harvesting

While harvesting
From this garden
Paradise,

Eternity,

Giving
Generously,

Greets me
Continuously.

And For You

Love
Speaking true

In heartbeats
Whispered

I want to be you

And for you
To be me too

Words

Hearing
Is echo-after-echo

Feeling is
Immortal

Close

How close
Can close be

Be that way
With me

As I love you
Love me

We Become

As you lay next to me
I fell your heartbeat

It's then

We

Become

Shade

Be from tree leaf
Or grass blade
There's a gift
In the cool
Of shade.

The Wellspring

With your love surrounding me
And the dark canopy of the night
Lit by the silver of starlight

All's ours

Sharing,
You move
And I move too

I love you

The Crape Myrtle

In awe
Of color
And form

Along the way
I stopped.

What a wonder
Seeing
The folded flowers
Covering
The crimson crape myrtle;

So many blooms,
So much color.

Branches
Curved by grace
Reaching:

The earth
Caring
And holding.

What a gift it be
This harmony;
Of form, color
And me.

Just Once More

Sometimes
It takes more
Than once
To get it right

Maybe twice,
Maybe more

Just once more
Before
The winter comes
Let's walk
Hand-in-hand

This time
As we walk
Let's not talk

Let's listen
To the sound
Of late autumn
Beneath our feet

And perhaps
To jays
Calling to one another
Saying, stay
By me

When Next We Meet

The next time
I come your way
I'll
Come
A bit nearer,
Talk
A bit dearer,
Love
A bit stronger,
Stay
A bit longer
And
Come to know you
Much
Much more;
When
Next
We meet.

Bloom
After Bloom

My small self,
My greater being,

I don't know how
They come,
      grow
        and go.

But, knowing
Is not consequential
Nor essential
For the story of life
To be written.

Or, for that matter,
For love to bloom
In this garden of life
Or in this little room.

I Love You

In a Dizzying World

In a world so dizzying
I find my balance
On garden walks.

Come with me,
Hand in hand.

Be Love

ABOUT THE AUTHOR

Inspired by nature and the beauty around him
Gary W. Burns started writing poetry at a young age.
Early on Gary was able to express his thoughts, ideas
and emotions through the vivid imagery of his verse.
His poetry has been published in various literary arts
journals, anthologies and magazines. He is the author
of 10 books of poetry. Through his poems Gary
shares his reflections on the many facets of life and
on the beauty of nature. The expressiveness of his
poetry has been enriched by his wide reading in
philosophy and psychology. He has traveled
throughout the world and has lived in numerous
countries, to include, Italy, Korea, Saudi Arabia and
Canada. He has also lived in Hawaii and several
other states. Currently, Gary makes his home in
Northern Virginia near the foothills of the Blue Ridge
Mountains.

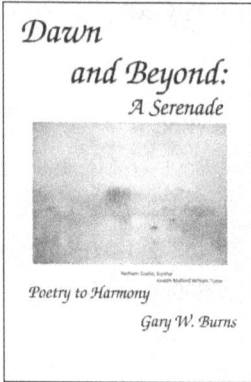

Dawn and Beyond: A Serenade
(Poetry to Harmony) (Due Out)
ISBN: 978-0-9827805-8-9 (Paperback)
ISBN: 978-0-9827805-9-6 (Hardcover)

Moments: This to the Next
(Poetry - Now and Eternity)
ISBN: 978-0-9845342-4-1 (Paperback)
ISBN: 978-0-9827805-1-0 (Hardcover)
ISBN: 978-0-9860900-9-7 (E-Book)

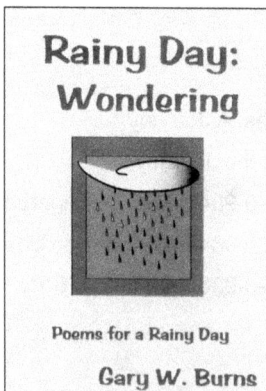

Rainy Day: Wondering
(Poems for a Rainy Day)
ISBN: 978-0-9845342-5-8 (Paperback)
ISBN: 978-0-9827805-2-7 (Hardcover)
ISBN: 978-0-9860900-7-3 (E-Book)

Available at WWW.TURNINGCORNERBOOKS.COM and where books are sold.

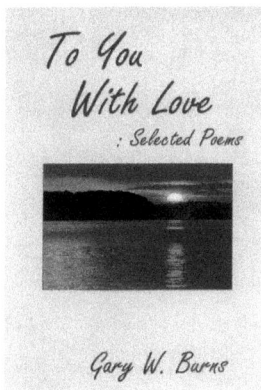

To You With Love: Selected Poems
ISBN: 978-0-9845342-6-5 (Paperback)
ISBN: 978-0-9827805-3-4 (Hardcover)
ISBN: 978-0-9860900-2-8 (E-Book)

Twilight: Awaking the Stars
(Poems of the Night's Light)
ISBN: 978-0-9845342-7-2 (Paperback)
ISBN: 978-0-9827805-4-1 (Hardcover)
ISBN: 978-0-9860900-6-6 (E-Book)

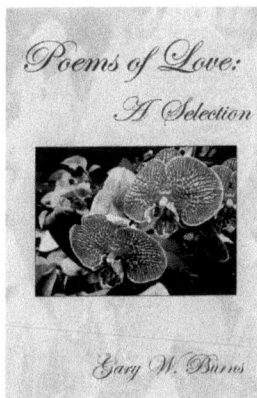

Poems of Love: A Selection
ISBN: 978-0-9845342-8-9 (Paperback)
ISBN: 978-0-9827805-5-8 (Hardcover)
ISBN: 978-0-9860900-5-9 (E-Book)

Available at WWW.TURNINGCORNERBOOKS.COM and where books are sold.

www.ingramcontent.com/pod-product-compliance
Lightning Source LLC
Chambersburg PA
CBHW072151020426
42334CB00018B/1953